BE
INSPIRED

Compilation Copyright © 2017 by Trish Madson
Illustrations Copyright © 2017 by Natalie Hoopes

Published by Familius LLC, www.familius.com

Familius books are available at special discounts for bulk purchases, whether
for sales promotions or for family or corporate use. For more information,
contact Familius Sales at 559-876-2170 or email orders@familius.com.
Reproduction of this book in any manner, in whole or in part, without
written permission of the publisher is prohibited.

Library of Congress Cataloging-in-Publication Data
2016959874   ISBN 9781942672913

Cover and book design by David Miles
Edited by Katie Arnold
Rainbow illustration on page 6 and frames
throughout licensed from Shutterstock.com.

10 9 8 7 6 5 4 3 2 1   Printed in China   First Edition

BE
INSPIRED

Compiled by Trish Madson

Illustrations by Natalie Hoopes

You'll never find a

rainbow if you're looking down.

CHARLIE CHAPLIN

For my part I know nothing with
any certainty, but the sight of the
stars makes me want to

dream.

VINCENT VAN GOGH

With the
new day
comes new
strength and
new thoughts.

ELEANOR ROOSEVELT

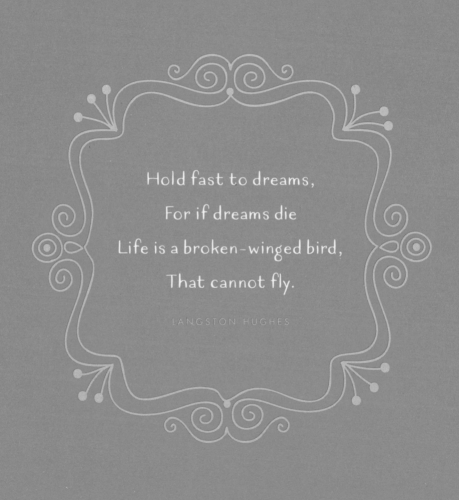

Hold fast to dreams,

For if dreams die

Life is a broken-winged bird,

That cannot fly.

LANGSTON HUGHES

It is good to love many things, for
therein lies the true strength, and
whosoever loves much performs
much, and can accomplish much, and
what is done in love is well done.

VINCENT VAN GOGH

The things you do for
yourself are gone when
you are gone, but the
things you do for others
remain as your legacy.

KALU NDUKWE KALU

You have power over your mind—
not outside events. Realize
this, and you will find

strength.

MARCUS AURELIUS

What you do makes a difference,
and you have to decide what kind of
difference you want to make.

JANE GOODALL

The only person who can

pull me down is

myself,

and I'm not going to let myself

pull me down anymore.

C. JOYBELL C.

All the effort in the
world won't matter if
you're not inspired.

CHUCK PALAHNIUK

I ask not for any crown
But that which all may win;
Nor try to conquer any world
Except the one within.

LOUISA MAY ALCOTT

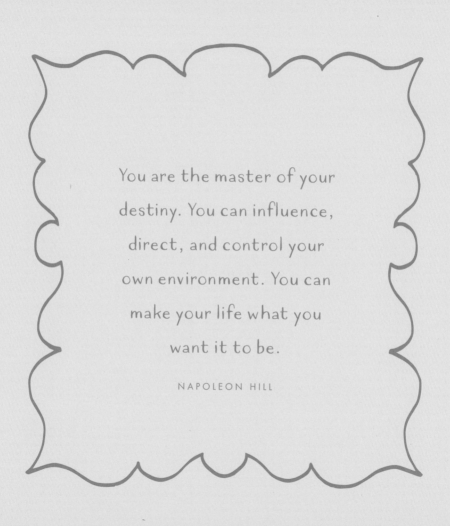

You are the master of your destiny. You can influence, direct, and control your own environment. You can make your life what you want it to be.

NAPOLEON HILL

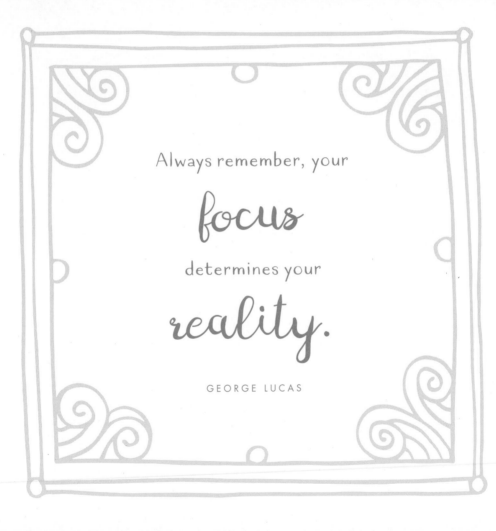

Always remember, your

focus

determines your

reality.

GEORGE LUCAS

Sometimes good things
fall apart so better
things can fall

TOGETHER.

JESSICA HOWELL

Be your own kind of amazing.

UNKNOWN

Stop and smell the roses.

ANONYMOUS

Reach high, for stars lie hidden
in you. Dream deep, for every
dream precedes the goal.

RABINDRANATH TAGORE

Obstacles

are things a person sees when

he takes his eyes off his goal.

E. JOSEPH COSSMAN

When the whole world is silent,

even one voice becomes powerful.

MALALA YOUSAFZAI

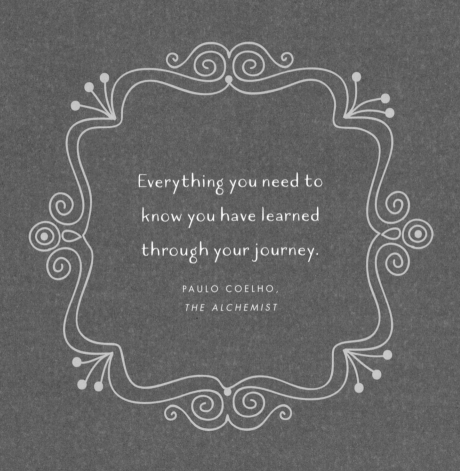

Everything you need to know you have learned through your journey.

PAULO COELHO,
THE ALCHEMIST

The probability that we may fail

in the struggle ought not to

deter us from the support of a

cause we believe to be just.

ABRAHAM LINCOLN

Inspiration is a guest that does not

willingly visit the lazy.

PYOTR ILYICH TCHAIKOVSKY

It's time to start living
the life you've imagined.

HENRY JAMES

You must give everything to
make your life as beautiful as
the dreams that dance in your
imagination.

ROMAN PAYNE

A dream

is not what you experience in

your sleep. A dream is that

which does not let you sleep.

A.P.J. ABDUL KALAM

Life is not measured by the number of breaths we take, but by the number of moments that take our breath away.

ANONYMOUS

To find what you seek
in the road of life, the
best proverb of all is that
which says: "Leave no
stone unturned."

EDWARD BULWER-LYTTON

Be yourself;

everyone else is already taken.

OSCAR WILDE

We but mirror the world. All the tendencies present in the outer world are to be found in the world of our body. If we could change ourselves, the tendencies in the world would also change. As a man changes his own nature, so does the attitude of the world change towards him. This is the divine mystery supreme. A wonderful thing it is and the source of our happiness. We need not wait to see what others do.

MAHATMA GANDHI

No one can make you feel inferior

without your consent.

ELEANOR ROOSEVELT

Life isn't about finding yourself.

Life is about creating yourself.

GEORGE BERNARD SHAW

It is good to have an end
to journey toward; but
it is the journey that
matters, in the end.

URSULA K. LE GUIN

He turns not

back who is

bound to a star.

LEONARDO DA VINCI

Keep away from people
who try to belittle your
ambitions. Small people
always do that, but the
really great make you
feel that you, too, can
become great.

MARK TWAIN

You may not control all the events that happen to you, but you can decide not to be reduced by them.

MAYA ANGELOU, *LETTER TO MY DAUGHTER*

The biggest adventure
you can ever take is
to live the life of your
dreams.

OPRAH WINFREY

What lies behind us and
what lies before us are
tiny matters compared
to what lies within us.

HENRY STANLEY HASKINS

If you can't fly, then run; if
you can't run, then walk; if
you can't walk, then crawl;
but whatever you do, you
have to keep moving forward.

MARTIN LUTHER KING JR.

The secret of health for both mind and body is not to mourn for the past, nor to worry about the future, but to live the present moment wisely and earnestly.

GAUTAMA BUDDHA

Though nobody can go back and make
a new beginning . . . anyone can start
over and make a new ending.

CHICO XAVIER

Kindness is a language
which the deaf can hear
and the blind can see.

MARK TWAIN

I don't think of all the
misery, but of the beauty
that still remains.

ANNE FRANK

Keep your face always
toward the sunshine—
and shadows will fall
behind you.

WALT WHITMAN

Dream as if you will live forever; live as if you will die today.

JAMES DEAN

Imperfection

is beauty, madness is genius,
and it's better to be absolutely
ridiculous than absolutely boring.

MARILYN MONROE

I have not failed. I've
just found 10,000
ways that won't work.

THOMAS A. EDISON

To be happy, you must

be your own sunshine.

C.E. JERNINGHAM

Positive Mind, Positive Vibes, Positive Life.

UNKNOWN

The higher we soar,

the smaller we appear to

those who cannot fly.

FRIEDRICH NIETZSCHE

Never look back unless
you are planning to go
that way.

HENRY DAVID THOREAU

Too often we underestimate
the power of a touch, a smile,
a kind word, a listening ear,
an honest compliment, or the
smallest act of caring, all of
which have the potential to
turn a life around.

LEO BUSCAGLIA

I trust that everything happens
for a reason, even if we are not
wise enough to see it.

OPRAH WINFREY

Go confidently in
the direction of
your dreams.

HENRY DAVID THOREAU

No act of kindness, no matter

how small, is ever wasted.

AESOP

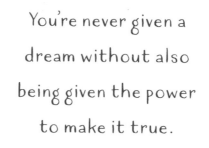

You're never given a
dream without also
being given the power
to make it true.

RICHARD BACH

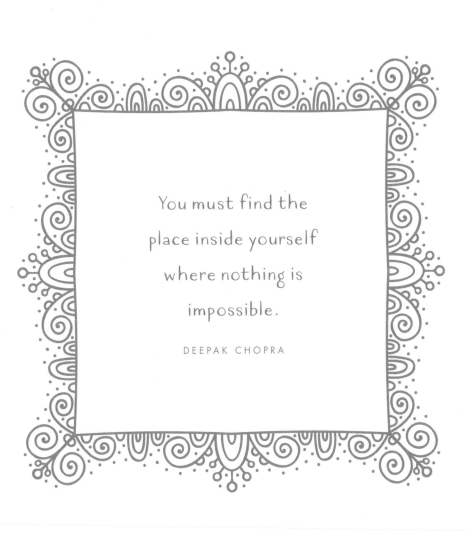

You must find the
place inside yourself
where nothing is
impossible.

DEEPAK CHOPRA

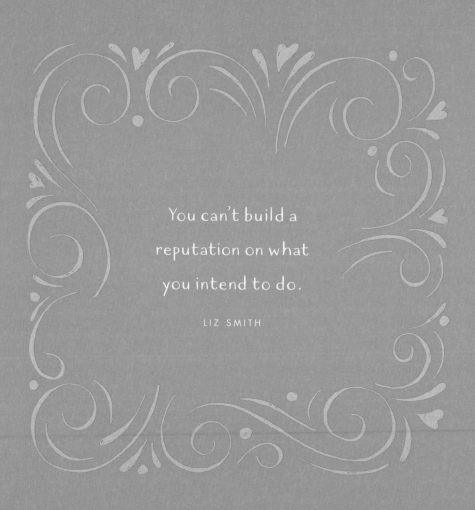

You can't build a
reputation on what
you intend to do.

LIZ SMITH

Do not let what you

cannot do interfere

with what you can do.

JOHN WOODEN

It's not what the goal is —

it's what the goal does.

ANONYMOUS

Winners

keep track of results and

losers keep track of reasons

. . . with equal intensity.

CHUCK COONRADT

Things that don't change remain the same. Things that remain the same quickly become obsolete.

GEORGE ODIORNE

I can live two
months on a good
compliment.

MARK TWAIN

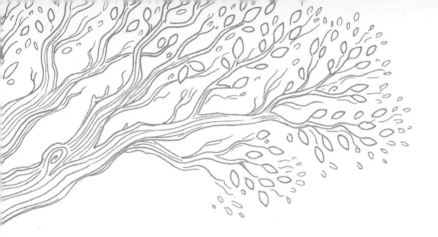

Everyone is a potential winner.

Some people are disguised as losers.

Don't let appearances fool you.

KEN BLANCHARD

Control is a delusion.

This is dangerous. You have

influence—not control.

CHRISTOPHER ROBBINS

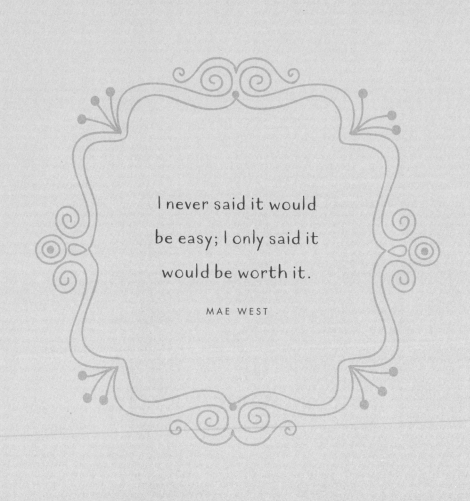

I never said it would
be easy; I only said it
would be worth it.

MAE WEST

Life

was meant to be lived, and

curiosity must be kept alive.

One must never, for whatever

reason, turn his back on life.

ELEANOR ROOSEVELT

When you arise in the morning, think of what a privilege it is to be alive, to think, to enjoy, to love . . .

MARCUS AURELIUS

Life has no remote . . .

GET UP AND

CHANGE IT

YOURSELF!

MARK A. COOPER

When each day is the same as
the next, it's because people
fail to recognize the good
things that happen in their lives
every day that the sun rises.

PAULO COELHO, *THE ALCHEMIST*

Whatever the mind
can conceive and
believe, it can achieve.

NAPOLEON HILL

Life is a journey, not a destination.

Some pursue happiness—

others create it.

ANONYMOUS

Start by doing what is necessary, then what is possible, and suddenly you are doing the impossible.

ST. FRANCIS OF ASSISI

To live

is so startling it

leaves little time for

anything else.

EMILY DICKINSON

The most important
decision you make is to
be in a good mood.

VOLTAIRE

All great
achievements
require time.

MAYA ANGELOU

This life is yours.

Take the power to choose what you want to do, and do it well. Take the power to love what you want in life, and love it honestly. Take the power to walk in the forest, and be a part of nature. Take the power to control your own life. No one else can do it for you. Take the power to make your life happy.

SUSAN POLIS SCHUTZ

The three great essentials to achieve anything worthwhile are, first, hard work; second, stick-to-itiveness; third, common sense.

THOMAS A. EDISON

There is no passion to be found playing

small—in settling for a life that is less

than the one you are capable of living.

NELSON MANDELA

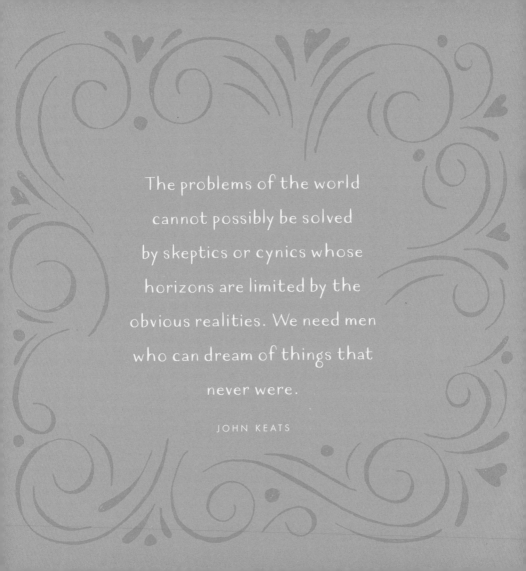

The problems of the world
cannot possibly be solved
by skeptics or cynics whose
horizons are limited by the
obvious realities. We need men
who can dream of things that
never were.

JOHN KEATS

It does not matter how long you are spending on the earth, how much money you have gathered, or how much attention you have received. It is the amount of positive vibration you have radiated in life that matters.

AMIT RAY

The beautiful journey of today can only begin when we learn to let go of

yesterday.

STEVE MARABOLI

I've had a lot of
worries in my life,
most of which
never happened.

MARK TWAIN

My past has not
defined me, destroyed
me, deterred me, or
defeated me; it has only
strengthened me.

STEVE MARABOLI

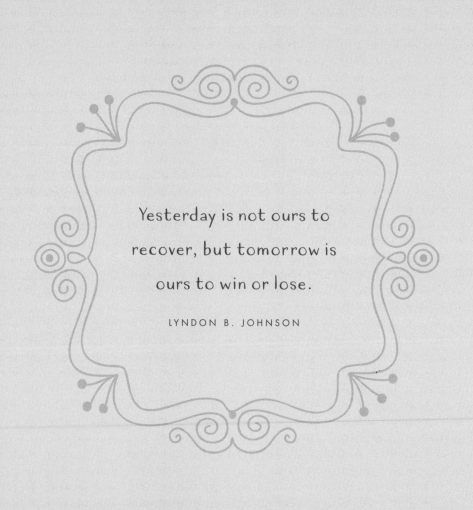

Yesterday is not ours to recover, but tomorrow is ours to win or lose.

LYNDON B. JOHNSON

I long to accomplish a great and noble task, but it is my chief duty to accomplish small tasks as if they were

great and noble.

HELEN KELLER

As a single footstep will not make a path
on the earth, so a single thought will
not make a pathway in the mind. To make
a deep physical path, we walk again and
again. To make a deep mental path, we
must think over and over the kind of
thoughts we wish to dominate our lives.

HENRY DAVID THOREAU

When you have exhausted all
possibilities, remember this:

you haven't.

THOMAS A. EDISON

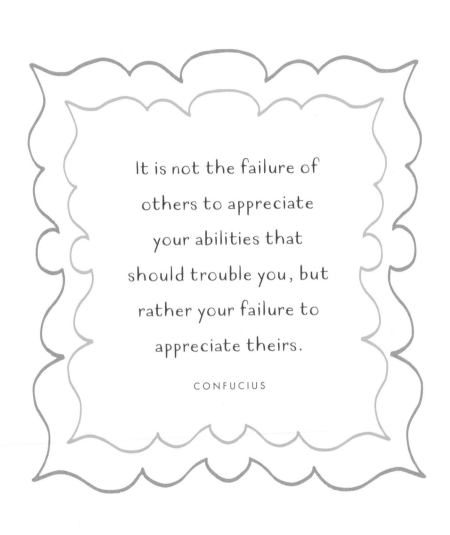

It is not the failure of others to appreciate your abilities that should trouble you, but rather your failure to appreciate theirs.

CONFUCIUS

What is now proved was once only

imagined.

WILLIAM BLAKE

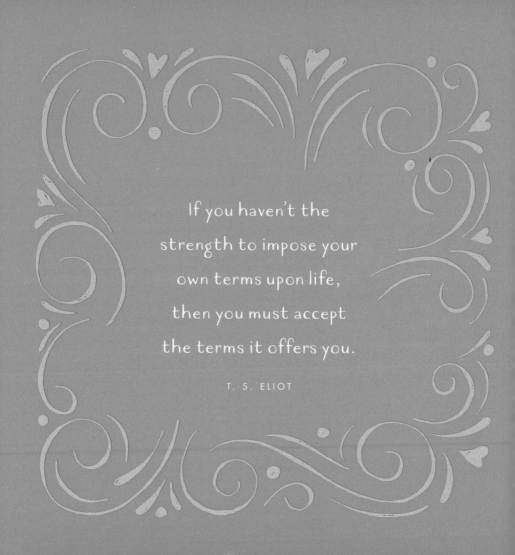

If you haven't the
strength to impose your
own terms upon life,
then you must accept
the terms it offers you.

T. S. ELIOT

Any intelligent fool can make things bigger, more complex, and more violent. It takes a touch of genius and a lot of courage to move in the

opposite direction.

E. F. SCHUMACHER

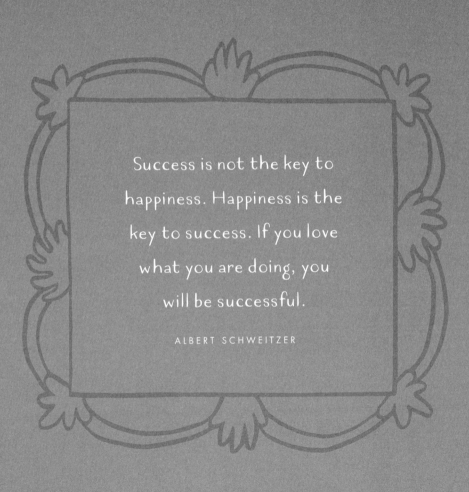

Success is not the key to happiness. Happiness is the key to success. If you love what you are doing, you will be successful.

ALBERT SCHWEITZER

It is amazing what you can
accomplish if you do not care
who gets the credit.

HARRY TRUMAN

We should not judge people
by their peak of excellence,
but by the distance they
have traveled from the point
where they started.

HENRY WARD BEECHER

Great things are not done by impulse, but by a series of small things brought together.

VINCENT VAN GOGH

Life is only as good as you make it.

UNKNOWN

Be the reason someone

smiles

today.

ANONYMOUS

Go and make interesting
mistakes, make amazing
mistakes, make glorious and
fantastic mistakes. Break
rules. Leave the world more
interesting for your being here.

NEIL GAIMAN

Difficulties

strengthen the mind as
labor does the body.

SENECA

Intellectual growth should commence at

birth and cease only at death.

ALBERT EINSTEIN

You can't go back and
make a new start, but
you can start right
now and make a brand
new ending.

JAMES R. SHERMAN

We don't receive wisdom; we must discover it for ourselves after a journey that no one can take for us or spare us.

MARCEL PROUST

A man who does not think for
himself does not think at all.

OSCAR WILDE

When you take risks, you learn that there will be times when you succeed and there will be times when you fail, and both are equally important.

ELLEN DEGENERES

Every great dream begins with a
dreamer. Always remember, you
have within you the strength,
the patience, and the passion
to reach for the stars to
change the world.

HARRIET TUBMAN

You are your problem and also your

solution.

UNKNOWN

Imperfection is Individuality.

ANONYMOUS

Don't find fault; find a remedy.

Anybody can complain.

HENRY FORD

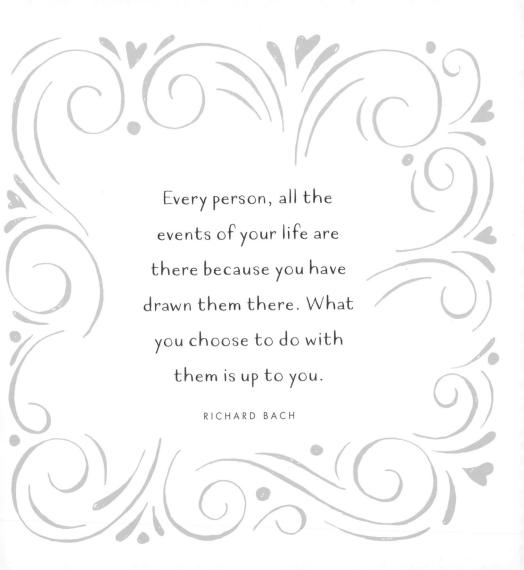

Every person, all the
events of your life are
there because you have
drawn them there. What
you choose to do with
them is up to you.

RICHARD BACH

Re-examine all you
have been told.
Dismiss what
insults your soul.

WALT WHITMAN

We judge ourselves by what
we feel capable of doing,
while others judge us by
what we have already done.

HENRY WADSWORTH LONGFELLOW

Courage

does not always roar. Sometimes
courage is the quiet voice at the
end of the day saying, "I will try
again tomorrow."

MARY ANNE RADMACHER

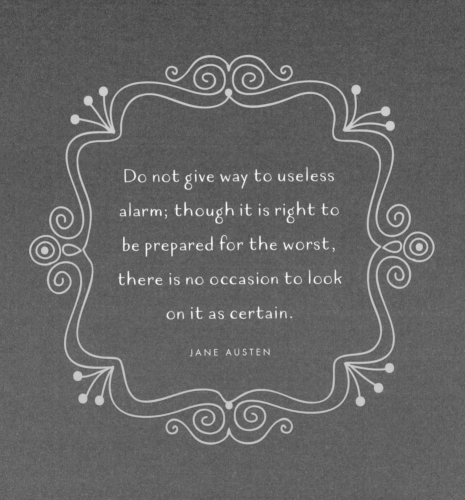

Do not give way to useless alarm; though it is right to be prepared for the worst, there is no occasion to look on it as certain.

JANE AUSTEN

The greatest discovery of any generation is that a human can alter his life by altering his attitude.

WILLIAM JAMES

Grace is the face that love wears

when it meets imperfection.

JOSEPH R. COOKE

Realize deeply that the

present moment is all

you will ever have.

ECKHART TOLLE

Your own positive future begins in this moment. All you have is right now. Every goal is possible from here.

LAO TZU

Courage and perseverance have a magical
talisman before which difficulties
disappear and obstacles vanish into air.

JOHN QUINCY ADAMS

My hope still is to leave the world a bit better than when I got here.

JIM HENSON

There is no failure

except in no longer

trying.

ELBERT HUBBARD

If we had no winter, the spring would not be
so pleasant: if we did not sometimes taste of
adversity, prosperity would not be so welcome.

ANNE BRADSTREET

What the mind can

conceive and believe,

and the heart desire,

you can achieve.

NORMAN VINCENT PEALE

We are what we believe we are.

C. S. LEWIS

The world is wide, and I will not waste my life in friction when it could be turned into momentum.

FRANCES E. WILLARD

The greatest pleasure in
life is doing what people
say you cannot do.

WALTER BAGEHOT

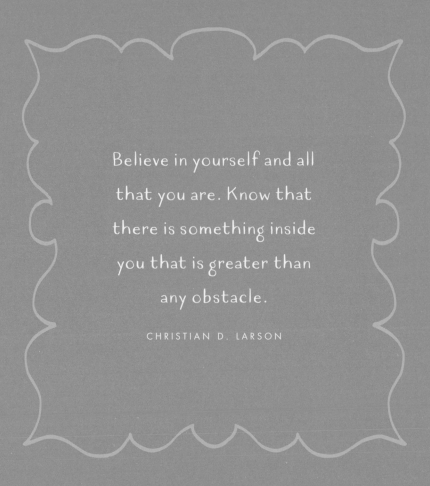

Believe in yourself and all
that you are. Know that
there is something inside
you that is greater than
any obstacle.

CHRISTIAN D. LARSON

There is force in the
universe, which, if
we permit it, will
flow through us and
produce miraculous
results.

MAHATMA GANDHI

Life is ours to be spent,

not to be saved.

D. H. LAWRENCE

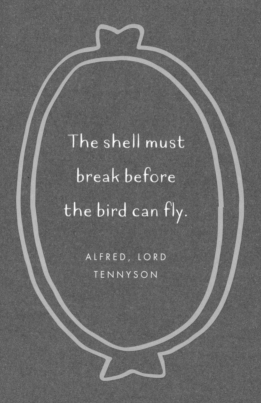

The shell must
break before
the bird can fly.

ALFRED, LORD
TENNYSON

Arrange whatever pieces come your way.

VIRGINIA WOOLF

Most don't deserve

your tears . . . and the

ones that do will never

make you cry.

T. RAFAEL CIMINO

To every problem, there is a
most simple solution.

AGATHA CHRISTIE

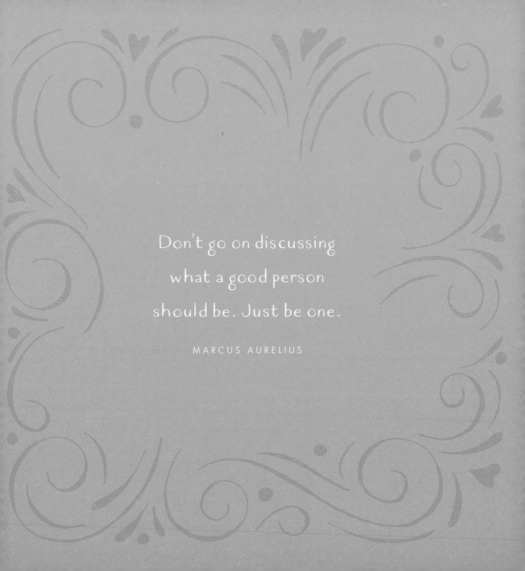

Don't go on discussing
what a good person
should be. Just be one.

MARCUS AURELIUS

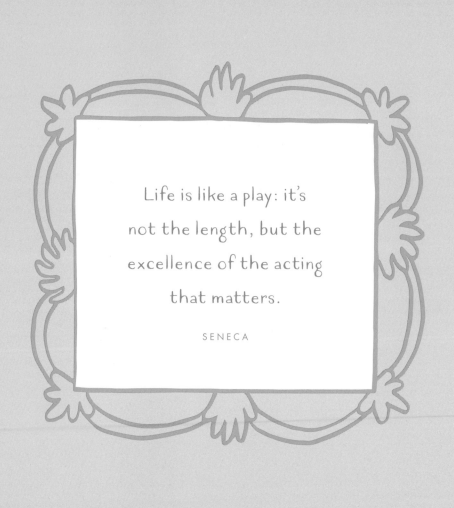

Life is like a play: it's
not the length, but the
excellence of the acting
that matters.

SENECA

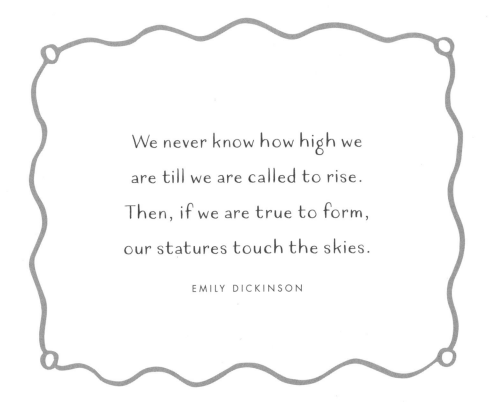

We never know how high we
are till we are called to rise.
Then, if we are true to form,
our statures touch the skies.

EMILY DICKINSON

If you don't
like the road
you're walking,
start paving
another one.

DOLLY PARTON

Happiness depends more on the

inward disposition of mind than on

outward circumstances.

BENJAMIN FRANKLIN

We are constantly

invited to be

who we are.

HENRY DAVID THOREAU

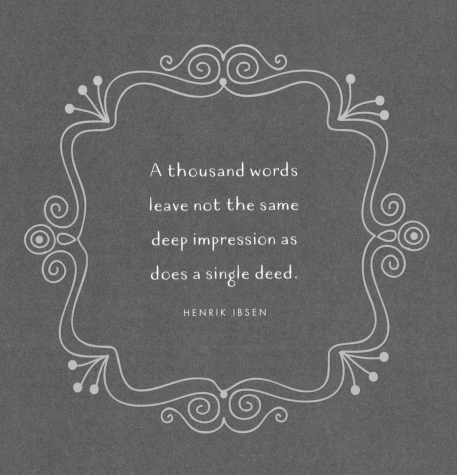

A thousand words
leave not the same
deep impression as
does a single deed.

HENRIK IBSEN

None of us will ever
accomplish anything excellent
or commanding except when
he listens to this whisper
which is heard by him alone.

RALPH WALDO EMERSON

It does not matter how long you live, but how well you do it.

MARTIN LUTHER KING JR.

In the midst of difficulty

lies opportunity.

OPRAH WINFREY

Accept whatever comes
to you woven in the
pattern of your destiny,
for what could more
aptly fit your needs?

MARCUS AURELIUS

Courtesy costs nothing,
but buys everything.

ALI IBN ABI TALIB

I am the
master of my
fate; I am
the captain
of my soul.

WILLIAM EARNEST HENLEY

Defeat is not the
worst of failures.
Not to have tried
is the true failure.

GEORGE E. WOODBERRY

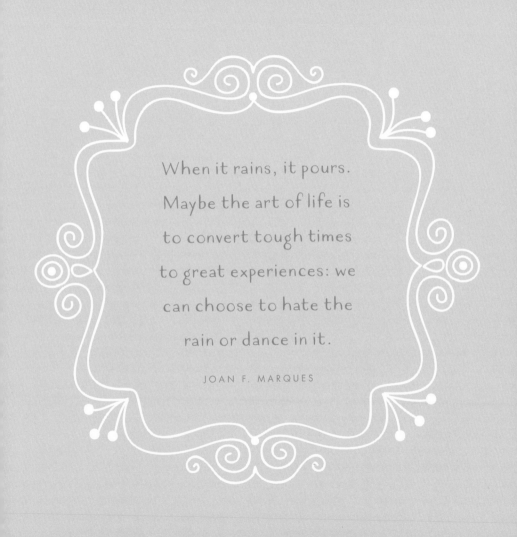

When it rains, it pours.
Maybe the art of life is
to convert tough times
to great experiences: we
can choose to hate the
rain or dance in it.

JOAN F. MARQUES

Do not lose hold of your dreams or
aspirations. For if you do, you may still
exist but you have ceased to live.

HENRY DAVID THOREAU

You get in life what you have the courage to ask for.

NANCY D. SOLOMON

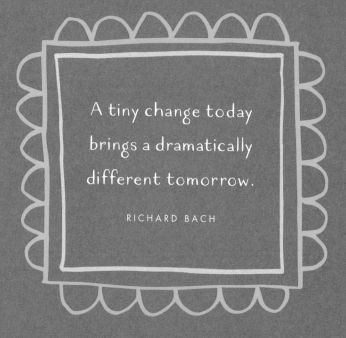

A tiny change today
brings a dramatically
different tomorrow.

RICHARD BACH

Scars show us where
we have been; they
do not dictate where
we are going.

DAVID ROSSI

The more we
value things,
the less we
value ourselves.

BRUCE LEE

Whether you know or not,

you are the infinite potential

of love, peace, and joy.

AMIT RAY

The life given us by
nature is short, but the
memory of a well-spent
life is eternal.

MARCUS TULLIUS CICERO

A bird is safe in its
nest —but that is
not what its wings
are made for.

AMIT RAY

What you do matters — but not much.

What you are matters tremendously.

CATHERINE DE HUECK DOHERTY

Exuberance is beauty.

WILLIAM BLAKE

Doing nothing for others is the undoing of ourselves.

HORACE MANN

To plant a garden is to
believe in tomorrow.

AUDREY HEPBURN

Who we are in the
present includes who we
were in the past.

FRED ROGERS

To accomplish great things, we
must not only act, but also dream;
not only plan, but also believe!

ANATOLE FRANCE

Arise, awake —

stop not until your

goal is achieved.

SWAMI VIVEKANANDA

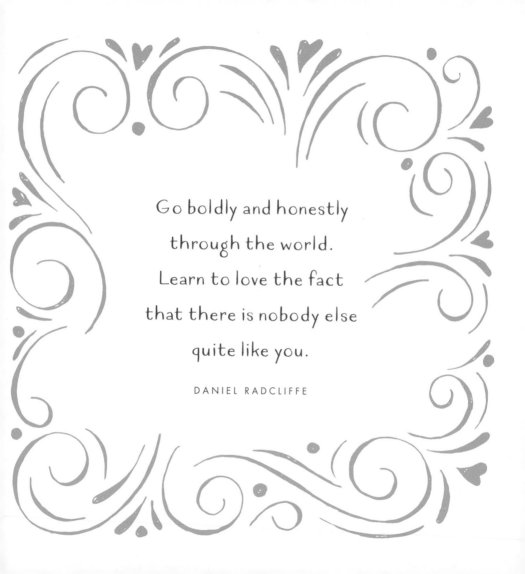

Go boldly and honestly
through the world.
Learn to love the fact
that there is nobody else
quite like you.

DANIEL RADCLIFFE

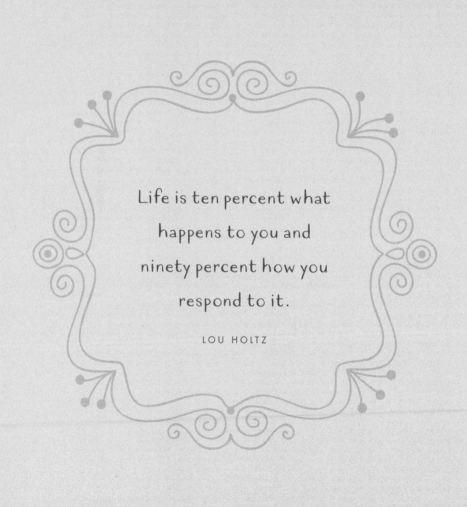

Life is ten percent what happens to you and ninety percent how you respond to it.

LOU HOLTZ

Your greatest self

has been waiting your whole life;

don't make it wait any longer.

STEVE MARABOLI

Every individual has a
place to fill in the world
and is important in some
respect, whether he
chooses to be so or not.

NATHANIEL HAWTHORNE

You are stronger than you know.

LORI OSTERMAN

When you're good at something, you'll tell everyone. When you're great at something, they'll tell you.

WALTER PAYTON

Differences are not intended to separate, to alienate. We are different precisely in order to realize our need of one another.

DESMOND TUTU

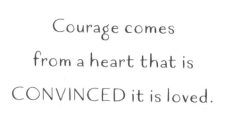

Courage comes
from a heart that is
CONVINCED it is loved.

BETH MOORE

Listen to what you know
instead of what you fear.

RICHARD BACH

When you lost sight
of your path, listen
for the destination in
your heart.

KATSURA HOSHINO

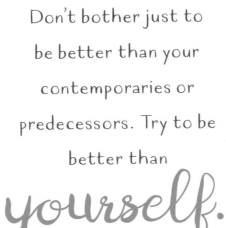

Don't bother just to
be better than your
contemporaries or
predecessors. Try to be
better than

yourself.

WILLIAM FAULKNER

To accomplish great
things, we must dream
as well as act.

ANATOLE FRANCE

It is necessary to hope, for hope

itself is happiness.

SAMUEL JOHNSON

What other people think
of me is not my business.

MICHAEL J. FOX

Only when I fall do I get up again.

VINCENT VAN GOGH

You make mistakes;

mistakes don't make you.

MAXWELL MALTZ

Trying is always enough.

PATRICIA BRIGGS

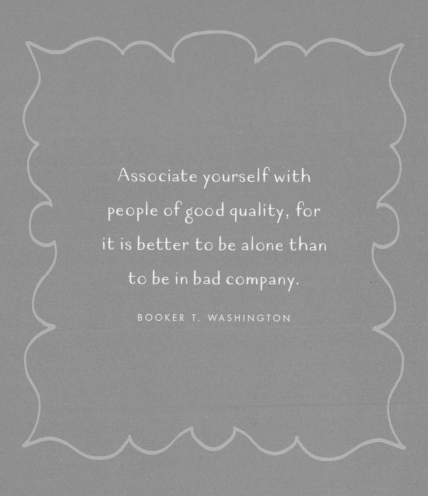

Associate yourself with
people of good quality, for
it is better to be alone than
to be in bad company.

BOOKER T. WASHINGTON

Make today worth remembering.

ZIG ZIGLAR

No day but today.

JONATHAN LARSON, *RENT*

Your life begins to
change the day you take
responsibility for it.

STEVE MARABOLI

Carpe diem.

[Seize the day.]

HORACE, *ODES*, 23 BC

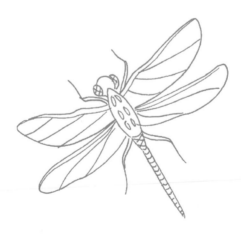

Attitude is everything.

CHARLES SWINDOLL

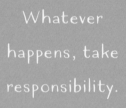

Whatever
happens, take
responsibility.

TONY ROBBINS

Know thyself.

SOCRATES

Never, never, never give up.

WINSTON CHURCHILL

Hope springs eternal.

ALEXANDER POPE

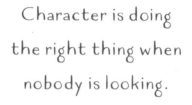

Character is doing
the right thing when
nobody is looking.

J. C. WATT

Anything can happen if you let it.

MARY POPPINS

Do it with passion or not at all.

ROSA NOUCHETTE CAREY

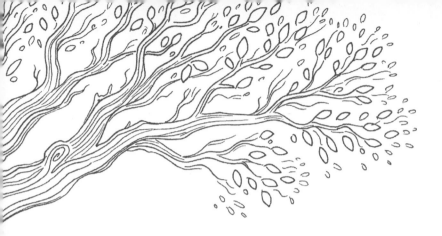

One positive thought in the morning

can change your whole day.

UNKNOWN

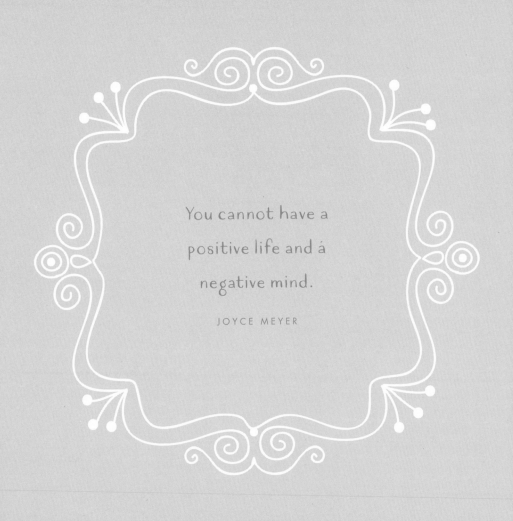

You cannot have a
positive life and a
negative mind.

JOYCE MEYER

Make your life a masterpiece,

you only get one canvas.

E. A. BUCCHIANERI

Let go of anything
that no longer serves
you, grows you, or
makes you happy.

UNKNOWN

You will face many
defeats in your life, but
never let yourself be

defeated.

MAYA ANGELOU

Nothing worth

having comes easy.

ANONYMOUS

ABOUT THE AUTHOR

Trish Madson is a lifelong book enthusiast with over 20 years experience in the publishing and entertainment industry. Her true passion is creating books that inspire and encourage children to learn while ultimately having fun. When she's not working on children's books, she enjoys reading, taking advantage of the amazing year-round outdoor activities in the Pacific Northwest, spending time with her family, and hanging out on the beach. You can find a complete history of Trish's work experience on LinkedIn.

ABOUT THE ILLUSTRATOR

Natalie Hoopes was born with a head full of wild ideas. She decided that only way to get them out was to be a painter. She graduated from Brigham Young University with a BFA in illustration. Her artwork has been published in the *The Friend*, *New Era*, and *Liahona* magazines. She currently lives in Utah with her husband and far too many books.